A Beginning-to-Read Book

Fall

by Mary Lindeen

NORWOOD HOUSE PRESS

DEAR CAREGIVER, The *Beginning to Read—Read and Discover* books provide emergent readers the opportunity to explore the world through nonfiction while building early reading skills. The text integrates both common sight words and content vocabulary. These key words are featured on lists provided at the back of the book to help your child expand his or her sight word recognition, which helps build reading fluency. The content words expand vocabulary and support comprehension.

Nonfiction text is any text that is factual. The Common Core State Standards call for an increase in the amount of informational text reading among students. The Standards aim to promote college and career readiness among students. Preparation for college and career endeavors requires proficiency in reading complex informational texts in a variety of content areas. You can help your child build a foundation by introducing nonfiction early. To further support the CCSS, you will find Reading Reinforcement activities at the back of the book that are aligned to these Standards.

Above all, the most important part of the reading experience is to have fun and enjoy it!

Sincerely,

Shannon Cannon

Shannon Cannon, Ph.D.
Literacy Consultant

Norwood House Press • P.O. Box 316598 • Chicago, Illinois 60631
For more information about Norwood House Press please visit our website at
www.norwoodhousepress.com or call 866-565-2900.
© 2016 Norwood House Press. Beginning-to-Read™ is a trademark of Norwood House Press.
All rights reserved. No part of this book may be reproduced or utilized in any form or by any
means without written permission from the publisher.

Editor: Judy Kentor Schmauss
Designer: Lindaanne Donohoe

Photo Credits:

Shutterstock, cover, 1, 8-9, 10, 11, 12-13, 14-15, 16, 17, 20-21, 22-23, 24-25, 26-27, 28-29; Phil Martin, 3, 4-5, 6-7; Dreamstime, 18-19 (Casadphoto)

Library of Congress Cataloging-in-Publication Data

Lindeen, Mary, author.
Fall / by Mary Lindeen.
    pages cm. – (A beginning to read book)
    Summary: "Fall is a special time of year. The leaves change colors, the weather gets cooler, birds fly south, and school starts. Find out about picking apples, Halloween, and all the things there are to like about fall. This title includes reading activities and a word list"–Provided by publisher.
    Audience: Grades K to 3.
    ISBN 978-1-59953-681-1 (library edition : alk. paper)
    ISBN 978-1-60357-766-3 (ebook)
    1. Autumn–Juvenile literature. I. Title.
    QB637.7.L56 2015
    508.2–dc23
                                                                                2014047649

Manufactured in the United States of America in Stevens Point, Wisconsin. 275N–062015

It is fall.

Fall comes after summer.

The leaves change color in the fall.

Some leaves are red.

Some leaves are yellow.

Some leaves are orange.

The leaves come down.

They are all over the ground.

Look at all the
leaves!

Run and jump in!

School starts in the fall.

You will meet your new teacher.

You will see your friends.

You will learn new things.

The air gets cool
in the fall.

People put on hats
and coats.

Some birds fly away to
warm places in the fall.

These geese are flying south.

Farmers harvest their crops in the fall.

This farmer is harvesting his corn crop.

You can pick apples
in the fall.

Yum, yum, yum!

You can pick pumpkins in the fall, too.

Some are small.

Some are very big!

What special day comes in the fall?

Halloween!

There is a lot to like about fall.

What do you like best?

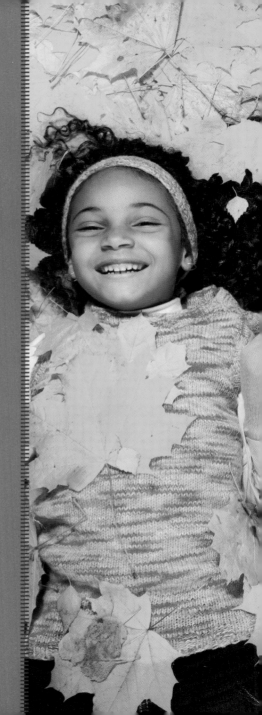

•• Reading Reinforcement ••

CRAFT AND STRUCTURE

To check your child's understanding of this book, recreate the following diagram on a sheet of paper. Read the book with your child, then help him or her fill in the diagram using what they learned. Work together to complete the diagram by writing the main idea of this book and several details relating to it:

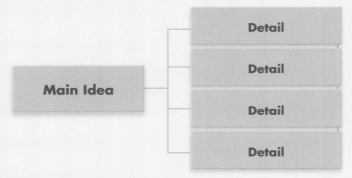

VOCABULARY: Learning Content Words

Content words are words that are specific to a particular topic. All of the content words for this book can be found on page 32. Use some or all of these content words to complete one or more of the following activities:

- Write each word and each definition on separate cards. Play a memory game by turning all cards face down and then turning them over to find matching pairs of words and definitions.

- Help your child make up sentences that use two or more content words.

- Ask your child questions that include one or more of the content words. Each question should begin with one of these words: *who, what, when, where, why,* or *how.*

- Help your child make associations between two content words. Pick any two content words, and have your child think of something these words have in common.

- Help your child make word cards: On each card, have him or her write a content word, draw a picture to illustrate the word, and write a sentence using the word.

FOUNDATIONAL SKILLS: Adjectives

Adjectives are words that describe nouns (people, places, things, and ideas); for example, *pretty*, *green*, and *four* are all adjectives. Have your child identify the words that are adjectives in the list below. Then help your child find adjectives in this book.

jump	leaves	special	silly	yellow
scary	dress	corn	warm	pumpkins

CLOSE READING OF INFORMATIONAL TEXT

Close reading helps children comprehend text. It includes reading a text, discussing it with others, and answering questions about it. Use these questions to discuss this book with your child:

- Which season comes before fall?
- What happens to the trees in the fall?
- What does fall mean for some kinds of birds?
- What are two things you know about fall?
- What might happen if farmers didn't harvest crops in the fall?
- What do you think about fall?

FLUENCY

Fluency is the ability to read accurately with speed and expression. Help your child practice fluency by using one or more of the following activities:

- Reread this book to your child at least two times while he or she uses a finger to track each word as you read it.
- Read the first sentence aloud. Then have your child reread the sentence with you. Continue until you have finished this book.
- Ask your child to read aloud the words they know on each page of this book. (Your child will learn additional words with subsequent readings.)
- Have your child practice reading this book several times to improve accuracy, rate, and expression.

··· Word List ···

Fall uses the 82 words listed below. *High-frequency* words are those words that are used most often in the English language. They are sometimes referred to as sight words because children need to learn to recognize them automatically when they read. *Content words* are any words specific to a particular topic. Regular practice reading these words will enhance your child's ability to read with greater fluency and comprehension.

High-Frequency Words

a	can	like	small	too
about	come(s)	look	some	very
after	day	new	the	what
air	do	on	their	will
all	down	over	there	you
and	get(s)	people	these	your
are	his	place(s)	they	
at	in	put	things	
away	is	school	this	
big	it	see	to	

Content Words

apples	crop(s)	harvest(ing)	pick	teacher
best	fall	hats	pumpkins	warm
birds	farmer(s)	jump	red	yellow
change	fly(ing)	learn	run	yum
coats	friends	leaves	south	
color	geese	lot	special	
cool	ground	meet	starts	
corn	Halloween	orange	summer	

··· About the Author

Mary Lindeen is a writer, editor, parent, and former elementary school teacher. She has written more than 100 books for children and edited many more. She specializes in early literacy instruction and books for young readers, especially nonfiction.

··· About the Advisor

Dr. Shannon Cannon is a teacher educator in the School of Education at UC Davis, where she also earned her Ph.D. in Language, Literacy, and Culture. She serves on the clinical faculty, supervising pre-service teachers and teaching elementary methods courses in reading, effective teaching, and teacher action research.